JESUS

JESUS

Mercy from God's Heart

Written, compiled, and edited by
Kathryn J. Hermes, FSP
and Christine Setticase, FSP

The Library of Congress has cataloged the earlier printing as follows:

Library of Congress Cataloging-in-Publication Data

Jesus : help in every need / compiled and edited by Kathryn J. Hermes and Christine Setticase.

p. cm.

ISBN 0-8198-3991-4 (pbk.)

1. God (Christianity)—Mercy—Meditations. 2. God (Christianity) — Mercy—Biblical teaching. 3. Jesus Christ—Biblical teaching. 4. Mercy—Meditations. 5. Spirituality—Christianity. I. Hermes, Kathryn. II. Setticase, Christine S.

BT153.M4J48 2010

242'.4—dc22

2010003563

Cover design by Rosana Usselmann

Cover art: Heinrich Hofmann, *Christ at Thirty-Three*, detail from *Christ and the Rich Young Ruler*, 1889.

ISBN 10: 0-8198-4015-7

ISBN 13: 978-0-8198-4015-8

Published by Pauline Books & Media, 50 Saint Pauls Avenue, Boston, MA 02130-3491. www.pauline.org.

Printed in the U.S.A.

Pauline Books & Media is the publishing house of the Daughters of St. Paul, an international congregation of women religious serving the Church with the communications media.

3 4 5 6 7 8 9 20 19 18 17 16

Contents

Introduction

Dear Reader,

Jesus says to you, "Come to me!" The Gospels are simply an elaboration on these three words: come to me. In his being born as one of us, living among us, and reaching out in healing, teaching, and saving lives, Jesus bends low to share the lot of us all. The condition for finding relief, Jesus says, is to come to him: "Are you tired? Worn out? Burned out.... Come to me. Get away with me and you'll recover your life. I'll show you how to take a real rest. Walk with me and work with me—watch how I do it. Learn the unforced rhythms of grace. I won't lay anything heavy or ill-fitting on you. Keep company with me and you'll learn to live freely and lightly" (Mt 11:28–30, *Message* translation).

If you are holding this book in your hand, you might be looking for the prayers for the Chaplet to the Divine Mercy, or the Twelve Promises of Our

Lord to Saint Margaret Mary, or information on the First Friday Devotion.

Why do we pray the Chaplet to the Divine Mercy or celebrate the Feast of Divine Mercy? Why do we keep the First Friday Devotion? Why do we want to consecrate ourselves and our families to the Sacred Heart of Jesus? Why do we want to know Jesus' promises? We want mercy for ourselves or others. We live inundated with expectations, schedules, parameters, and red tape when we desperately need help. And we often evaluate others according to how they measure up to our criteria. We may cut people off from a relationship, make demands on them, and at times refuse to forgive and move on. Into this world, our world, your world and mine, comes Divine Mercy, the Teacher and Lord who simply loves us, accepts us, and invites us to come to him.

As you read this book and pray the prayers it contains, I invite you to be aware of the movements of your soul. Jesus will love you, invite you, and perhaps even challenge you to make some changes in your life: in the way you think, in the things you choose, and in the way you love. As you experience Jesus, the Shepherd who leads you to restful pastures, bending low to refresh you, you will begin to see ways in which you can shepherd others. Jesus will show you how to bend low to serve and care for them in quiet ways. The ripple of the Master's mercy and love will begin to transform your life and bring healing gifts to those around you. His way will become your way so that through you, others will find their way to mercy.

Sister Kathryn James Hermes, FSP

Mercy in the Scriptures

I waited patiently for the LORD;
he inclined to me and heard my cry.
He drew me up from the desolate pit....
He put a new song in my mouth,
a song of praise to our God.
Many will see and fear,
and put their trust in the LORD.

— PSALM 40:1–3

The Story of the Father's Mercy

The Old Testament gives us many stories of the Father's mercy. From personal stories such as those of Isaiah, or Hannah, or Jeremiah, to the great narratives of the Israelites concerning Abraham, Moses, and the prophets, we always find God's mercy.

The story of the Father's mercy could be seen as having three phases that unfold from the Book of Genesis through the Gospels: creation (God's first gift of love that causes us to be); covenant (when God claims a people as his own and promises fidelity to them); and incarnation (when God's love takes on flesh and steps into our history, to do for us himself what we couldn't do for ourselves).

Creation: Genesis 1–2

The story begins with the dawn of creation. God takes pleasure in bringing forth an extravagant variety of things: earth, sun, moon, plants, animals, oceans, forests. And then God creates man and woman in his likeness. God commits himself not just to creating, but also to maintaining his creatures, which need the breath of his spirit every moment, day after day, for an entire lifetime. Without God we would cease from existing.

A special Hebrew word describes this love of the Father: *rahamim*. This word denotes the deep bond that exists between mother and child, which results in a love that is wholly gratuitous, unearned, unable to be repaid. It is a love that can't help but flow out of a mother's heart. In creating us, in sustaining us, in forgiving us, God shows us this love.

Rahamim describes God's *merciful* love shown to us when we refuse God's love again and again, from those first days in the Garden to this very day. Despite such love at our beginning, we are so feeble in returning that love. We are easily swayed to discover "good" where God is not, and to be bored where God is. We forget the One who made us, and desire the thrill of what we can get away with, what we can become, what we can do on our own. God's love for us is marked by goodness and tenderness, patience and understanding that extend through the generations. As we live with, sustain, and forgive others, we learn to love as God loves us.

Covenant: Exodus 13–15, 19

Another aspect of the Father's love is denoted by the Hebrew word *hesed*. This word is connected to God's rescue of the Israelites from slavery in Egypt that they might worship him at Mount Sinai. God reached down and led the children of Abraham, Isaac, and Jacob out of slavery in Egypt. He heard their cries and acted on their behalf through mighty deeds and wonders. God brought them to the foot of Mount Sinai, that sacred mountain where he would make a covenant with them through his servant Moses.

In this covenant, he would be their God and they would be his special people—not because they were better than anyone else, but because he had decided to pity them and take them as his own. He made himself responsible for their protection and well-being and they, for their part, were to listen to his commandments and wholeheartedly obey them.

Hesed denotes an attitude of goodness between two parties, an attitude so profound that they are faithful to each other because of a deep interior commitment. Their fidelity to each other becomes fidelity to themselves because they have pledged themselves to each other. The covenant God made with Israel on Mount Sinai was an incredible promise of fidelity on the part of God to his creatures. The covenant had a sort of juridical or legal sense. When Israel broke the covenant and strayed from God, which happened over and over in the long course of salvation history, God no longer was "legally bound" to be faithful to his part of the covenant. But he remained faithful. It was precisely when the relationship was broken that *hesed* was revealed most deeply: it showed a love stronger than sin and a grace more powerful than betrayal.

Incarnation: Luke 2

The Father's mercy responded to the deep longing of his people by entering into creation, into the fabric of human living, in God's Son made flesh. Jesus forgave sinners, healed the sick, reached out in mercy, and spoke to us of love. He taught the way of poverty and simplicity, which does not boast in arrogant pride but rather has mercy even on the unjust. Jesus' every word and deed are direct revelations of the intentions of God, of the love and mercy of the Father's heart. Believing in Jesus means believing that love has been made present in the world, that love is more powerful than evil. It means standing beneath the cross, believing in God's mercy for ourselves and for the world. Committing to follow Jesus is to allow oneself to be "remade," to become a "new creation," to become selfless, to be Christ-like love poured out for others.

Jesus Christ: Mercy Made Visible

One of the Beatitudes that Jesus proclaimed in the Sermon on the Mount is precisely about mercy: how fortunate the merciful (cf. Mt 5:7). Those who practice the Beatitudes imitate God. Those who have taken on the life of mercy live, think, and desire as does God, who is mercy itself.

Mercy is a movement that bestows life and love on another, that bends low wherever it finds misery. It restores the one who is suffering to the image originally intended for him or her by God himself. Mercy means offering life. Jesus taught us mercy through his parables and through his actions.

The Parable of the Good Samaritan: Luke 10

Mercy means to be shaken at the plight of another. One of the most profound parables Jesus told about mercy is the parable of the Good Samaritan. Christ himself is the Good Samaritan to the human race. God's mercy is poured without reserve into the heart of his Son. Christ descends to earth, to become man, to reach down and pick us up from the side of the road where we have been left for dead—weak, wounded, and ill. He comes, not to walk past us in arrogance or indifference, but to nurse us to health with divine tenderness, to restore us to the image and likeness of God in which we were first created. The Son of God has cast his lot with us. The Samaritan took the wounded man left for dead on the side of the road to the nearest hotel. He promised to pay whatever was necessary for the man to be made well. This reflects the love of Jesus, who has done and will do whatever is necessary to save us from sin and death.

Jesus and the Woman Caught in Adultery: John 8

Mercy is a powerful aspect of love. It prevails over sin and infidelity. A woman has been caught in the act of adultery and dragged before a group of men so that justice should be served—she is shamed, humiliated, exposed. Jesus, unlike us, however, is not interested in punishment as much as he is in winning over the love and fidelity of the sinner.

Jesus bends down to write in the sand. Could it be that he does not want to humiliate the woman further by looking at her, so exposed and humiliated? Or is he trying to get down to her level, if she were crouching on the ground trying to make herself invisible, in an act of compassion and pity? In any case, when the crowd persists in asking how the woman should be treated, Jesus simply states: "Let anyone among you who is without sin be the first to throw a stone at her." One by one the men leave, uneasily, aware that they also have hidden sins they don't want exposed to merciless public scrutiny. Only two sentences are recorded of the conversation between Jesus and the woman, but perhaps Jesus said more: words of kindness, gently but firmly inviting the woman to change her life. Conversion blossoms under the working of love and the presence of mercy in our world.

The Parable of the Prodigal Son: Luke 15

Love becomes true mercy when it stretches beyond the norms of justice. In the parable of the Prodigal Son, the father is often in the background. The son who flees his former life, taking his inheritance, casting off the relationship and authority of his father for the wild life of a young rebel—this youth's colorful story is what usually grabs our attention. Perhaps we more easily identify with him, at least a little.

However, this parable on the lips of Mercy himself may have been meant to teach us more about the father. How patient is this father who waits day after long day, week after week, month after endless month for his child's return. How loving is this parent who, when the son returns, does not reciprocate the ill treatment and insult he had been shown by his child. How great-hearted he is to see beyond the mistaken choices his son has made for an illusory happiness that could not last. The father is patient with his son, knowing his difficult experience would form him into a man. His son had made a choice. He had made a mistake. He would suffer for it, and, with hope, he would learn from it. Absolutely he would be welcomed home, no longer a naive boy but a wiser man, ready to truly enter into relationship with his father—man to man.

Jesus Asks Peter, "Do You Love Me?": John 21

Peter, the impetuous disciple whose faults are scrawled across the pages of the Gospels, brings the Parable of the Prodigal Son to life. We see Peter betraying Jesus, running to save his own life, hiding and leaving Jesus alone with only John and the women beneath the cross—he who had boasted that he would die before betraying the Lord. How could Peter face the Master again? But on the shores of the lake, around a campfire, at a breakfast prepared by the Risen One, Peter experienced for all of us the reality of the Parable of the Prodigal Son. It is not just a story. The words of Jesus reveal the heart of the Father. "Simon … do you love me?" "[D]o you love me?" "Do you love me?" Thrice the question pierces Peter's heart. No longer does he boast of his love. He knows his weakness, how easy it is to fall into self-protective modes of behavior. Quietly he answers yes, because he does indeed love the Master. Jesus does not utter one word about the betrayal, the hiding, the running away. He simply tells Peter he has work for him to do and to follow him. This is his judgment—a judgment made in love. Do you love me? Then that's enough. Come follow me. Put your love into practice.

The Parable of the Merciless Servant: Matthew 18

Peter had finally found the central knot of mercy. He needed mercy, and he knew it. The Parable of the Merciless Servant, however, teaches us what to do with this most personal of discoveries. A servant owes his master a large sum of money and has been forgiven his debt. He is spared from being sold into slavery with his family to pay it off. Immediately after this he meets someone who owes him a small amount of money. Showing no mercy, he has him imprisoned until he pays back what he owes. The beatitude that tells us we are fortunate and blessed if we show mercy is the key to unlocking this parable. What we need the most, we must give to others. We depend on the merciful love of God. We have no other recourse, for we owe a debt that we could never pay. God doesn't tell us to work extra hard to pay it. He forgives it. But because we have received mercy, we need to show others the mercy we have most needed ourselves.

Jesus Begs for Our Mercy: Matthew 18

In the Parable of the Merciless Servant we could focus on the judge who has the power to decide whom to forgive and whom to condemn. But Jesus, perhaps, wants us to focus on the third and most hidden person in the parable—the person who begs for mercy and who is refused mercy by his fellow servant. This last person represents Jesus, who is always a beggar, asking for our mercy. We have been forgiven. Mercy has been shown us. But how often we neglect to show mercy toward Jesus and to remain in solidarity with he who suffered and died to save us. He rescues us, as it were, from a burning building and transfers us safely to the kingdom of light and love. "Listen! I am standing at the door, knocking..." (Rev 3:20). It is up to us to let him in. It is up to us to show him mercy. "As you did it to one of the least of these ... you did it to me." The human heart is capable of this most wondrous attribute of God: mercy. It is our greatest dignity to practice a love for others that overreaches justice and becomes mercy, thus showing mercy to the Lord.

Saint Paul: "God Has Shown Me Mercy": Acts 22, 1 Timothy 1, Ephesians 2

Outside of the Gospels, only one person in the New Testament narrates his autobiographical reflections on what God has accomplished in him: Saint Paul. That story revolves entirely around the merciful way Paul has been treated, the love he has been shown in being purchased for God, and the fire of devotion that burns in his heart for Jesus.

In the Acts of the Apostles, Paul's encounter with Jesus on the road to Damascus is recounted three times. In several passages of his letters, Paul reflects on its meaning. Jesus had to get in Paul's way and stop him, because Paul's whole life was intent on one thing: getting rid of those Israelites who believed in Jesus as the Messiah. Paul believed that these people were jeopardizing the identity of the Israelite people. He was on his way to Damascus to continue his zealous efforts when God revealed his Son to him, as he recounts:

> While I was on my way and approaching Damascus, about noon a great light from heaven suddenly shone about me. I fell to the ground

> and heard a voice saying to me, "Saul, Saul, why are you persecuting me?" I answered, "Who are you, Lord?" Then he said to me, "I am Jesus of Nazareth whom you are persecuting." … I asked, "What am I to do, Lord?" The Lord said to me, "Get up and go to Damascus; there you will be told everything that has been assigned to you to do." (Acts 22:6–8, 10)

Paul refers to this meeting with the Lord Jesus in terms of mercy:

> … I was formerly a blasphemer, a persecutor, and a man of violence. But I received mercy because I had acted ignorantly in unbelief, and the grace of our Lord overflowed for me with the faith and love that are in Christ Jesus. The saying is sure and worthy of full acceptance, that Christ Jesus came into the world to save sinners—of whom I am the foremost. But for that very reason I received mercy, so that in me, as the foremost, Jesus Christ might display the utmost patience, making me an example to those who would come to believe in him for eternal life. (1 Tim 1:13–16)

From that moment on, Paul became part of the community of those who believed in Jesus, crucified and risen, the promised Messiah. Those whom he had formerly persecuted he now collaborated with, seeking to spread near and far the story of God's mercy to us in Christ, because he had experienced it firsthand.

Paul made it clear, again and again, to those who followed him that they were also called and blessed out of mercy. It was a gift. Not because they were better than others, nor because they were smarter, but because God decided to call them.

> But God, who is rich in mercy, out of the great love with which he loved us even when we were dead through our trespasses, made us alive together with Christ—by grace you have been saved—and raised us up with him and seated us with him in the heavenly places in Christ Jesus, so that in the ages to come he might show the immeasurable riches of his grace in kindness toward us in Christ Jesus. For by grace you have been saved through faith, and this is not the result of your own doing; it is the gift of God—not the result of works, so that no one may boast. For we are what he has made us, created in Christ Jesus for good works, which God prepared beforehand to be our way of life. (Eph 2:4–10)

Paul understood that because he had been called he was now sent as an ambassador of reconciliation to proclaim the message of mercy.

Mercy Revealed Through the Centuries

There is therefore no condemnation for those who are in Christ Jesus. For the law of the Spirit of life in Christ Jesus has set you free from the law of sin and death... If God is for us, who is against us? He who did not withhold his own Son, but gave him up for all of us, will he not with him also give us everything else?

— Romans 8:1–2, 31–32

The Earliest Depiction of Jesus' Mercy in Art

In early Christian art Jesus is depicted only symbolically. The canonical Gospels do not describe what Jesus looked like. During the first 300 years of the Church's life, the persecutions that flared made it dangerous to be a Christian. Because of the need for secrecy, images of Jesus were purposely ambiguous. So the Christians turned to symbol.

One such symbol was the dolphin, which appears in the Roman catacombs from the late second to the early fourth century. This image arises from its reputation of saving sailors at sea. As a Christian symbol it depicts Jesus as the savior of people tossed on the sea of life.

The Christians also used the important image of the fish. This image predates Christianity as a symbol of well-being and survival because it represented food. Christians saw many more layers of meaning in the symbol of the fish. It recalled the miracle of the loaves and the fishes (a Eucharistic image), and the miraculous catch of fish (symbolizing Jesus' presence and power). The Greek word for fish—*icthus*—is an acronym of *Jesus Christ, Son of God, Savior.*

The Christians also used the image of a young man carrying a lamb or goat on his shoulders. In the earliest depictions this image was probably not considered as a portrait of Jesus but as a symbolic representation of the Savior. A Greek sculpture from 525 B.C. known as the Calf-Bearer is one of the images underlying the depiction of the Good Shepherd in the catacombs. Closer to the time of the early Church, a sculpture of an old woman carrying a lamb to market on her shoulders or under her arm was popular. The sculpture probably evoked sympathy for the woman who had to sell her lamb to survive. The image of the Good Shepherd reverses this image. The young man is not carrying the sheep to be slaughtered for his own survival. Instead, he has become the sheep who has given his life for *our* survival.

The Gospel also describes the Good Shepherd as laying down his life for his sheep, throwing a party when he finds one of the flock who has run away, and protecting the flock from danger and false shepherds.

The *Via Crucis*

The Gospels linger over the narrative of the betrayal and death of Jesus, keeping alive the events of his last days. Several chapters of each Gospel narrate both with the tragic details of Jesus' passion and the immense surprise of his resurrection. His rising filled the blackened future of the apostles and the world with a new and splendid hope.

Archaeological findings from as early as the second century indicate worship was offered in the place where Christ had been buried. A hundred years later, an embryonic form of the Way of the Cross took place on Golgotha. According to records, three holy buildings were constructed there. Processions with the chanting of psalms were conducted in commemoration of the death of Jesus. In the Middle Ages, replicas of the holy places connected to the death of the Savior began to be set up in Europe. Those who couldn't go to Jerusalem to walk in the footsteps of the Savior could walk the Way of the Cross locally.

In the late Middle Ages, the teaching and writings of Saint Bernard of Clairvaux (d. 1153), Saint Francis of Assisi (d. 1226), and Saint Bonaventure of Bagnoregio (d. 1274) infused into this practice of walking with Jesus on the way to Golgotha, a contemplative devotion and an expression of deep gratitude for the gift of mercy, universal reconciliation, and peace given to us by the Lamb of God.

Toward the end of the sixteenth century, the number of "stations" became fixed at fourteen. The Way of the Cross continues to be popular. Each Good Friday the Pope celebrates the Way of the Cross in the Colosseum in Rome.

Bernard of Clairvaux: A Personal Love for a Very Human Jesus

Saint Bernard dominated the spirituality of the first half of the twelfth century. Before him, Christian spirituality emphasized Christ's majesty and glorious divinity. However, this French aristocrat turned Cistercian monk was captivated by the Savior's humanity. As a young man Bernard had studied poetry and excelled in literature. So as a young abbot he wrote and preached in a way that instilled in his readers and fellow monks a more experiential knowledge of Jesus and personal love for him. Instead of meditating on the glory of the Incarnation, Bernard led people to visualize concrete images: to picture a real manger, to see the babe shivering in the cold, to hear the angels singing with joy in the night, to stand in the crowd watching Jesus cure the lepers, or to kneel beneath a real cross and hold the feet of the dying Lord in their hands. For Bernard, Jesus is not only a historical figure, but he is also alive here and now. He is personally in love with each of us and acts on our behalf with power. The image of Christ in glory dominated the early Middle Ages. Bernard was captivated by the lowliness of the Savior. Christ's passion was for him a real and wholly personal experience.

Bernard's spirituality emphasizes love. God desires to recapture our love by drawing us to love his Son who has become human like us. This love that grows when the heart is freed from other lesser loves results in our becoming one with God and God becoming one with us. Bernard called it a mystical marriage in which God is united to the creature and penetrates to the depths of our being. In this mystical experience the soul is enraptured by love, emptied of self, and lost wholly in God.

Julian of Norwich: God Can Never Be Angry with Us

Julian (1342–c. 1416) was a great mystic, but little is known of her early life. In fact, Julian is probably not even her real name. She lived in Norwich, England, and spent much of her life as an anchorite, living a vowed life by herself in a small room attached to a parish church. Lady Julian is most known for her book *Revelations of Divine Love.* It describes a series of visions through which God revealed to her his unconditional love for us in Jesus Christ.

Julian's writings convey a truly remarkable message for the time in which she lived. The medieval Church emphasized God's wrath and condemnation of sinners. She lived during the Black Death that killed seventy-five million people worldwide. It is estimated that 30 to 60 percent of Europe's population succumbed. The Black Death led to unstable social conditions, oppression of the poor, high taxes, bad harvests, and general unrest. The major insurrection in 1381, known as the Peasants' Revolt, marked the beginning of the end of serfdom in medieval England. Unrest and confusion affected the Church too. The papacy was in exile in Avignon, France. Large numbers of clergy and religious died during the plague, seriously hampering the Church's ability to minister to people.

Although we are 600 years distant from Julian's medieval world, the epidemics, economic upheavals, wars and insurrections, troubles in the Church, social instability, and oppression of the poor make her times seem eerily similar to our own. Into this world, the unsophisticated Julian comes with a remarkable message that God has no wrath toward us. Instead, God is good and God is peace. God wishes us to live rooted in love, so God cannot become angry with us. Julian calls him a courteous God.

Though it seems that if sin had not entered the world humanity would have been pure and happy, the Lord told Julian that sin was inevitable. Nevertheless, in the famous words of *Revelations of Divine Love,* "All shall be well, and all shall be well, and all manner of things shall be well."

Margaret Mary Alacoque: Devotion to the Sacred Heart of Jesus

Saint Margaret Mary was born at L'Hautecour in Burgundy on July 22, 1647. Despite poor health, she entered the Visitation Order at twenty-three years old with an intense love for Jesus in the Eucharist. A year later she received her first vision of Jesus. He showed her his Sacred Heart and invited her to make her abode in his side. Jesus continued to appear to the young nun and asked her to be his instrument in revealing the love of his Sacred Heart to the world. Jesus told her that his love for humanity was so intense that it could no longer contain itself and needed to spread through the world. Her mission was to establish the devotion to his Most Sacred Heart, and he revealed twelve promises for those who practice this devotion. The heart of this devotion is found in welcoming the love of Jesus into our hearts and loving him in return. Popular practices such as the Nine First Fridays have sprung from this devotion.

Margaret Mary's superior and some of her sisters in community would not believe in her visions and treated her with hostility. Theologians judged her visions to be delusions. But Jesus promised Margaret Mary that he would send someone to help her.

Soon after, Saint Claude de la Colombière, an experienced Jesuit, became the confessor to the nuns. Margaret Mary immediately recognized him as the helper Jesus had promised to send her. Claude was convinced the visions were authentic, and adopted the teaching himself. He wrote a book on devotion to the Sacred Heart that was read aloud to the nuns. Later, when Sister Margaret Mary was serving as novice mistress, she encouraged devotion to the Sacred Heart among the novices. A chapel was built in honor of the Sacred Heart and the devotion began to spread throughout France.

In 1765 Pope Clement XIII officially recognized the devotion to the Sacred Heart of Jesus. The liturgical Feast of the Sacred Heart of Jesus was approved in 1856, and Margaret Mary was canonized by Pope Benedict XV in 1920.

The devotion to the Sacred Heart is also practiced in the family with the enthronement of the Sacred Heart in the home. The enthronement is the recognition of the kingship of the Sacred Heart in the Christian family. When the image of the Sacred Heart is enthroned and then venerated in the home, it leads to a way of life of devotion and love. The image of the Sacred Heart reminds the family of the immense love of Jesus for us.

Faustina of Poland: The Devotion to the Divine Mercy

In 1905 Saint Faustina was born in Poland to a poor family and baptized with the name Helena. While she was growing up, she stood out from the other children for her obedience, prayer, and sensitivity to the poor. At the age of twenty she entered the Congregation of the Sisters of Our Lady of Mercy and took the name Sister Mary Faustina. She led a simple, hidden life, but one of deep union with God. Only her superiors were aware of this.

The supernatural world was as real to Faustina as the world around her. God gave her unique spiritual gifts: visions, bilocation, prophecy, the reading of souls, revelations, the invisible stigmata (hidden from others but nonetheless real), and a remarkable familiarity with the saints and the souls in purgatory. It was as if Faustina could see through the veil that separates time and eternity.

Saint Faustina is most remembered, however, in connection with the Divine Mercy. Jesus made Faustina an apostle or secretary of his mercy. He commissioned her to tell the world that he did not want to punish the human race but rather to heal it, like a loving parent who draws a child close to his or her heart. Faustina's mission also included begging mercy for humanity today through the new forms of devotion to the Divine Mercy that Jesus was giving to the world. These forms included such practices as veneration of the image of the Divine Mercy, celebrating the Feast of the Divine Mercy, praying the chaplet to the Divine Mercy, and prayer at the Hour of Mercy (3:00 PM). At the heart of the devotion is the invitation to entrust one's life entirely to God with childlike trust, which expresses itself in fulfilling his will and in showing mercy toward one's neighbor.

Jesus told Faustina that his mercy was available to everyone. The more one trusts in that mercy, the more mercy one will receive. We can also trust in God's mercy for others. In particular Jesus gave her a short prayer that could be said at the Hour of Mercy for the conversion of sinners. Faustina recorded all this in her diary, which she kept at the request of Jesus and her confessors.

According to Jesus' wish, the Feast of Divine Mercy is celebrated on the first Sunday after Easter. On this day God is to be worshipped for his tender mercy to humanity. The readings for the liturgy on this day speak of the mercy that has been available to humanity from the beginning of the world, offered gratuitously to all. However, Jesus also wanted this day to be a day of grace for all people, especially for sinners.

Jesus attached great promises to this feast, especially that those who receive Communion on the Feast of the Divine Mercy will receive complete forgiveness of sins and punishment. Everyone may obtain any grace for the asking, if the request is compatible with God's will. Saint Faustina recorded in her diary that Jesus told her:

> I desire that the Feast of Mercy be a refuge and shelter for all souls, and especially for poor sinners. On that day the very depths of my tender mercy are open. I pour out a whole ocean of graces upon those souls who approach the fount of my mercy. The soul that will go to Confession and receive Holy Communion shall obtain complete forgiveness of sins and punishment. On that day are open all the divine floodgates through which graces flow. Let no soul fear to draw near to me, even though its sins be as scarlet.[1]

The Feast of Divine Mercy devotion was celebrated unofficially in many places for some years. On April 30, 2000 (Divine Mercy Sunday that year), Pope John Paul II canonized Saint Faustina and officially designated the Sunday after Easter as Divine Mercy Sunday. He also decreed that a plenary indulgence may be obtained by those who observe the Feast of Divine Mercy. Today millions of people have taken up the mission of mercy given us by Faustina. Pope John Paul II, who had brought this devotion to the greater awareness and celebration of the Church, died during the vigil of

---

1. Sisters of Our Lady of Mercy, *Jesus, I Trust in You* (Boston: Pauline Books & Media, 2002), pp. 20–21.

Divine Mercy Sunday in 2005. We continue to rely on Saint Faustina as a constant reminder of the message to trust in Jesus' endless mercy, and to live mercifully toward others.

James Alberione: Devotion to Jesus as Divine Master and Shepherd

A young Italian seminarian, Blessed James Alberione, spent the night between the nineteenth and twentieth centuries in Eucharistic adoration, praying for the new century about to begin. The explosion of media and communication technology was on the horizon, but he was already keenly aware of the influential power of the printed word and cinema. Alberione was pastorally concerned about the masses of confused people whose lives would be increasingly shaped by the media they consumed. All this need for healing welled up in his heart and was met with the quiet words he heard from Jesus that night, "Come to me.... I will refresh you...." Bring the world to Jesus. In Jesus they will find light, strength, wisdom, real love. Years later, again in Eucharistic adoration, he heard the words of Jesus: "Do not fear. I am with you. From here (the Eucharist) I will enlighten you. Be sorry for sin."

Alberione began the Pauline Family to bring the Church from the sacristies and schools into the world, to bring God into the lives of people wherever they are. By using newspapers, magazines, radio programs, DVDs, music albums, books, and any other media, the priests, sisters, brothers, and lay members seek to reach every person on earth. The Pauline Family brings the Gospel to everyone by using the communications technology that embeds our whole life. Speakers, presses, cameras, radio waves, TV stations, and computers are employed to reach the greater mass of people who, as in Jesus' time, find themselves so often like sheep without a shepherd (cf. Mk 6:34).

To Alberione, Jesus revealed his desire to be honored by all as the Master and Shepherd who nourishes, guides, instructs, and forms the entire life and personality of the disciple. The human person finds in Jesus as Master a divine teacher to whom he or she can bring all the weaknesses of mind, will, and heart for healing. Addictions, prejudices, lack of faith, or disordered loves can all be brought to the Lord. Jesus will transform our weakness so that we adopt his way of thinking, choosing, and loving.

Alberione wrote: "The stronger of the two elements assimilates the weaker one. Jesus Christ replaces man, so to speak: 'I live now not with my own life but with the life of Christ who lives in me' (Gal 2:20). It is a moral, intimate, and real transforming union...."[2] This healing requires several things: to know Jesus Christ; imitate Jesus Christ, love Jesus Christ. That is, let Jesus live in our minds, hearts, and will, in such a manner that he dominates our entire beings. Frequent reading of the Word of God and reception of the Eucharist are essential means to this transforming union. "It is in Communion that our natural life is replaced by the divine life of Jesus Christ. Grafted onto Jesus we will produce supernatural fruits. We will speak and think as Jesus did, live of Jesus, die with Jesus. We will have no other ideal than to be a living image of Jesus Christ."[3]

"The jewel which we must graft into our soul, so that it may give good, abundant, and beautiful fruits, is the Eucharist. Divine grafting! This precious gem transforms the plant. First we were proud, then we become humble; first avaricious, then detached; first sensual, then spiritual.... In the soul that nourishes itself on the Eucharist the fruits

---

2. Charism Committee, *The Following of Christ the Master in the Intuition of the Founder* (Boston: Pauline Books & Media, nd), p. 35.

3. Ibid.

of the Holy Spirit are produced. Saint Paul writes, 'The Spirit brings...: love, joy, peace, patience, kindness, goodness, trustfulness, gentleness, and self-control' (Gal 5:22)." [4]

The Feast of the Divine Master is celebrated by the Daughters of St. Paul and the Pauline Family on the last Sunday of October.

---

4. Ibid., p. 28.

What Does Mercy Mean for Us Today?

[T]he fruit of the Spirit is love, joy, peace, patience,
kindness, generosity, faithfulness, gentleness, and
self-control.... If we live by the Spirit,
let us also be guided by the Spirit.

— Galatians 5:22, 25

Acts of Mercy Form a Civilization of Love

John Paul II's 1980 encyclical *Dives in Misericordia* (*On the Mercy of God*) is the ideal guide to transforming society and human relationships through mercy. It addresses something very fundamental to our fragile existence, especially in a world marked by violence, force, and insecurity. It is human to rely on justice, punishment, and law to maintain a safe world—personally and internationally. John Paul II, however, proposes something greater than fear and security. He calls us to a love that is based on the love of the Father and of Jesus: a love stronger than sin, more powerful than betrayal, deeper than fear.

We hold in our hands power over one another: we can "pull the plug" and hasten another's death; we can sue one another and deprive one another of livelihood and future; we can directly take part in hurting one another through terrorist acts and smaller, but no less devastating, attacks on another's dignity. We have become a threat to one another.

Those most susceptible to fear, those less protected, are most vulnerable to this threat.

In *Dives in Misericordia,* John Paul II offers the hope and possibility of fashioning a different world, one that is more human. This world is not built on power, retribution, and lawsuits, but on relationships and forgiveness. Forgiveness is at the crux of such a civilization, and many find it the most difficult element to understand, accept, and practice. However, only forgiveness will show that love is in the world and that love is more powerful than evil.

Without the warmth of true forgiveness, we would be reduced to all of us demanding our due. When "my rights" become paramount, selfishness takes over. Concern for justice masks manipulation for personal gain, and our demands create a permanent state of conflict. This touches deeply upon the mystery of evil, which each of us has to confront in life. The husband whose wife leaves him and their children for the sake of a lucrative career or another romance, the woman whose business partner embezzles the company's funds, the friend whose kindness is misunderstood and whose trust is betrayed.... We understand the mystery of evil only when we embrace suffering and open ourselves to mercy, which is always in some way beyond our comprehension. Mercy is and will always remain a mystery, understood only when practiced.

Jesus requires Peter to forgive "seventy-seven times" (Mt 18:22), meaning he must forgive everyone every time. Jesus does not mean that the requirements of justice are no longer observed. He doesn't call us to indulge evil or turn our eyes away and let it go on. He doesn't ask us to accept injury, insult, and scandals without a word. Forgiveness requires reparation and compensation. Such forgiveness brings about justice on a level higher than a simple securing of "my" rights.

God's Love Overcomes Our Shame

In the sanctuary of our consciences we often struggle with guilt or shame. We remember past falls or abuse done to us; we struggle with present sins. We may worry about death and set up obstacles between us and where we want to be. We are so used to living in a world of scarcity, in a climate of litigation, in a society where we need to market ourselves, prove ourselves, look out for ourselves. Today's religious and political atmosphere draws clear lines about who's right and who's wrong, what's right and what's wrong. Too many times we are alone with our stories.

The pages of Scripture, however, tell us about a God who loves his chosen people with a love much like that of a spouse. Spousal love is generous, ecstatic, life-giving. It never runs out. It unites and does not divide. God as spouse offers us more than what we find in a fiercely competitive world. As a spouse, God reacts strongly to continued betrayal and infidelity, but for this reason he also pardons and takes Israel back at the first sign of repentance. In fact, when God asks the prophet Jonah to preach a message of conversion to the Ninevites, Jonah immediately gets on a ship going in the opposite direction. He knows that if the Ninevites show the smallest sign of conversion God would immediately change his plans to punish them and show them compassion instead. And that is exactly what happened. Scripture describes the love and tenderness of God in numerous places: from the *Song of Songs,* to the forgiveness of Mary Magdalene, to the mercy shown to Saint Paul. To Moses God declared that he was a "God merciful and gracious, slow to anger, and abounding in steadfast love and faithfulness" (Ex 34:6).

God's anger is continuously overcome by his tenderness and generous love. The prophets in the

Hebrew Scriptures and the apostles in the New Testament encourage people to appeal for mercy and to count upon it. Ultimately God cannot hate and be angry with the one to whom he has given himself. Love, by its very nature, will not allow it. We realize our mistakes, but God never proposed self-blame to anyone in the Scriptures. He called to conversion, but he never paralyzed anyone with accusation and guilt. Instead he wants us to present ourselves to him just as we are, that he might love us into what he would have us be.

We Can Trust God

God created us solely because he wanted us to exist. He saved us from our own sinful confusion when we couldn't save ourselves. He loved you and me into being and sustains us in life at every moment because he loves us. The Bible is like a "paper trail" of God's mercy. If we ever begin to wonder and question, we need only to open the Scriptures. The Gospel of Luke is a great place to start, since it is the Gospel that recounts the most parables and stories of God's mercy.

We can trust God to turn evil into good. Natural, personal, and national catastrophes shake our security. We seize on ways to make ourselves feel safe, to return things to normal. If we look around, however, we can discover many ways in which God is present to us even in the midst of the evil: people show remarkable unexpected integrity or charity; people grow strong and blossom in the wounded and seemingly dead places of their lives; someone forgives a drunken driver who has killed a brother; another goes to the funeral of a man who has shattered his family by murdering his children. As time goes by the cross evolves gradually into resurrected glory, even if the pain and sorrow don't entirely disappear.

Sometimes we can try to manipulate situations or circumstances to get what we think we need. God, however, has the long-range view of our lives. To get to the place where we will be the happiest, to become the person we really are, he knows just the right amount of sunshine and shadow we need. We can trust that God has our best interests at heart. As any good parent knows, too much candy isn't healthy for children, no matter how much they may want it. Each act in our lives is also a training ground for a Christ-like, generous, and whole life. Sometimes training grounds are like classrooms, and other times they are like boot camp. But in either case, the one in charge of the training has a goal for the trainees that will fulfill them in unexpected ways.

We can trust that even if it seems God is delaying to save us, he never leaves us. We want God to rescue us whenever we feel out of control, vulnerable, or tempted. And we usually want it *now*. However, often God holds back a quick rescue because the struggle opens up every inch of our being to receive more of his divine grace. God wants more for us than we could ever desire for ourselves. We may focus on quick fixes, but God sees the big picture. He knows all that he wants for us, all that we can be. He refuses to jettison the future for the sake of immediate satisfaction. His mercy runs deeper than our understanding.

We would ruin a plant if we tried to make it taller by pulling on it right after it breaks its way through the earth. Similarly, God would "ruin" his project in us if he weren't as patient as a gardener, waiting for us to develop naturally and to gradually prepare for the fullness of divine life.

God knows what it's like not to receive mercy. In the Garden of Olives, the night before he died, Jesus cried out to his Father for mercy, for a reprieve, for a change of plans. Judas had left the Passover supper just a few hours earlier to finalize the details for handing Jesus over to the authorities.

But even more deeply, Jesus knew that his hour had come, an hour of glory, yet at the same time an hour of shame and immense pain. He crumbled beneath the darkened sky, shaking, in a bloody sweat as he imagined the events of the following day. He prayed that if it were possible, the cross would be erased from his destiny.

We often forget to connect the dots. Jesus begged his Father for mercy, that the fire of love that God had for the world would find some other way to express itself. Jesus was alone with the weight of humanity squarely upon his shoulders. The Father didn't take the cup of suffering from his Son, and Jesus embraced the Father's plan for our redemption, giving his life in place of ours.

His three trusted apostles slept that night, oblivious to the sufferings and loneliness of their Master. Like them, countless people through the centuries have been ignorant of what Jesus has done for them or have shown indifference to Jesus.

Jesus understands when we offer prayers that seem to go unanswered, or when we tremble beneath an especially heavy cross. Jesus cares when we feel isolated, when others around us don't realize or even care about what we suffer, unable to show us compassion and mercy in our moment of deepest need.

On the cross, Jesus cried out that he felt abandoned, alone, no longer connected to the loving Father who had been but a breath away for his whole life. The darkness shrouding the cross invaded his soul. Jesus knows what abandonment is like, the deepest dregs of loneliness. He embraced the Father's desire so that we would know that there is no dark place in our lives that he has not experienced before us and for our sake.

We Can Face the Darkness and Find Compassion

Often we are too afraid to face the darkness. We run from our inner pain and build ourselves up to mask our fear. We cover over the holes in our heart with self-judgment or the judgment of others. Fear and blame lead to a culture of angry, reactive behavior and destructive words.

This cycle created by running from the pain consists of layers of emotion, which are usually as obvious and uncontrollable as tornadoes and thunderstorms. Fear, loneliness, anger, hurt, sadness, and at the deepest level, despair, cause us to keep up appearances, throw ourselves into work, manipulate the truth, boss others around, or play the victim.

By learning to pause for a moment and see our circle of perception within the larger circle of God's Providence, we can move away from being a victim. We will be able to see the cycle created by fear and blame.

We learn from Jesus, who is mercy itself, that the road to compassion is to face the inner darkness and to walk through life exactly as it is. We learn to pause long enough to step outside of the patchwork quilt of automatic thoughts, feelings, and stories through which we try to make sense of our lives. As we offer our own hearts the gift of compassion, we will be able to welcome others into our circle of compassion.

The Sacrament of Reconciliation

[The Lord] does not retain his anger forever,
because he delights in showing clemency.
He will again have compassion upon us;
he will tread our iniquities under foot.
You will cast all our sins
into the depths of the sea.

— Micah 7:18–19

A Special Gift from a Loving God

Simply put, God doesn't think or act the way we do. How else could we explain God's limitless mercy and love? We only need to ask for it with a repentant heart, and God totally and completely forgives us all our sins and offenses. This God truly sees the good in each and every one of us. This Father searches for any of his children who stray, and if we ever doubt this, reading the marvelous Parable of the Prodigal Son (Lk 15) will set us straight.

Indeed, many psychologists have wished for a healing device as effective as the sacrament of Reconciliation (confession). In just one session, we are given a brand new start, a new beginning. We should allow ourselves to experience the peace that this sacrament offers and not give in to the temptation to say, "Oh, no, my sin is so great that I am beyond redemption." That simply isn't true—accept the Father's gift of peace, which he desires to give you in this sacrament.

Sorrow and Trust

Father Michael Scanlon recounts his experience traveling in a small aircraft caught in a hailstorm:

> I thought I had only a few minutes to live, so I turned to the Lord and prayed, "There are many things in my life which I wish I hadn't done … and there are many things that I wish I had done … I'm sorry! I trust you with everything and with whatever is left of my life!" And I had such an experience of peace, light, hope, and the presence of the Lord that I didn't care whether the plane crashed or not. I have never forgotten that moment. The Lord's mercy and forgiveness are so great, they envelop you. I felt like the good thief being told, "This day you'll be with me in paradise."[5]

That simple prayer, "I'm sorry and I trust you with everything and with whatever is left of my life," is the central axis of the sacrament of Reconciliation: sorrow and trust. Once you have been forgiven through the words of the priest, allow trust to enter your soul. Be at peace and do not let doubt enter. If you have confessed your sins with a sincere heart, you do not have to fret over whether

---

5. Michael Scanlon, in *Jesus According to...*, ed. Edd Anthony, OFM (Boston: Pauline Books & Media, 1992), pp. 143–144.

you had the exact wording or even if you forgot to mention a minor fault or sin.

Four Simple Steps

There are four simple steps to this sacrament. (See page 98 for a detailed explanation of the rite.)

1. We take some time to prepare ourselves to celebrate the sacrament of Reconciliation. A good way to begin is to reflect on how God has shown his love to us since our last confession. It is when we are rooted in this love that we are able to have true sorrow for having offended God. We could pray a Psalm of wonder at God's love or read a passage from the Gospel. We review our thoughts, attitudes, actions and behavior, desires and affections, asking the Holy Spirit to help us see where we have not lived as true Christians, those who have put on the mind and life of Christ. We then express sorrow to the Lord for what we have done or have failed to do, for not having responded to the love we have been shown.

2. After spending some time in reviewing our actions from the time of our last reception of this sacrament (often called the "examination of conscience"), we tell our sins and faults to the priest

(prayers for the sacrament of Reconciliation are on page 96). We do this in complete confidence that the priest is representing Jesus and will maintain total secrecy about whatever we confide to him. We express our sorrow by means of an "act of contrition," which can be a memorized prayer or our own words that express sorrow. In declaring our remorse for sins, we are also voicing our intention not to repeat our offenses.

3. The priest who hears our confession gives us a penance that we perform after we leave the confessional. It may be the recitation of specific prayers, a brief meditation on a spiritual thought, or a charitable act.

4. We receive absolution (forgiveness) by means of the prayer that the priest recites over us. This is a moment of great freedom, knowing that Jesus has fully pardoned us for our sins and offenses and given us a new beginning.

Always remember that the priest is "standing in" for Jesus, who is there to welcome and embrace you with a loving and accepting heart. Your sin(s) will not overwhelm Jesus or his representative. This is the definition of total and absolute forgiveness—it is not the way of the world, but of a God who sacrificed his only Son so we could be set free from the bonds of sin.

Many parishes post a time when a priest is scheduled to be in the reconciliation room awaiting anyone who may wish to go to confession. (This information can be found in the parish bulletin or parish Web site.) Alternatively, an appointment for confession can be scheduled by calling the rectory. If for any reason you wish to remain anonymous, tell this to the priest when you make your appointment and ask to meet him in the reconciliation room. You might want to choose this latter option if you have something to confess that embarrasses you. Keep in mind that the priest has heard many confessions and that nothing we say in confession is going to surprise or shock him. If it has been many years since your last confession and you are not certain of the exact time, you can estimate the time and say, "it has been at least five years (or ten years, etc.) since my last confession." If you have forgotten how to go to confession, you could tell that to the priest and he will walk you through it.

From Lists to Conversation

Over time we mature in how we approach this sacrament. Though often in the beginning stages of going to confession we produce lists of things we have done wrong, in time it can give way to a conversation with Jesus about what he desires of us. Questions such as: Where have I felt a desire for something more in my life? What have I felt moved to do for others in ways that are out of the ordinary scope of my behavior? Has a movie or song or book struck me deeply with a realization about myself or God or others? Do I feel an attraction to a greater integrity, compassion, and charity in my relationship with myself or others? In all this has God been trying to invite me to something more in life? What would that look like? How am I gradually opening myself to this new avenue of trust and compassion?

Confession can be a consistent stepping-stone to personal transformation if we ask: What is God doing in my life? What am I doing that "seconds" his action, and what in me is resisting his invitation? Bringing this to Jesus in confession strengthens, clarifies, and opens up the way before us. Every celebration of the sacrament is new because God is always doing something new. We take our cue from God.

Frequent reception of the sacrament of Penance makes it easier to live the Christian virtues. Why? Because each time we receive a sacrament, we receive an infusion of grace. We receive this gift through the merits of Jesus' passion and death. His redeeming act was not just a "one time deal," but we continue to reap and enjoy the benefits of his mercy each time grace is bestowed on us.

Stories of Mercy

[E]veryone who thirsts,
come to the waters;
and you who have no money,
come, buy and eat!
Come, buy wine and milk
without money and without price....
Incline your ear, and come to me;
listen, so that you may live.

— Isaiah 55:1, 3

Sister Bernadette R., New York

When I was in Los Angeles, one day I received a call from my father. He told me that my grandfather, who lived in Wisconsin, was close to death. Other family members who were with my grandfather weren't as concerned, however, because they thought he would rally as he had done countless times before. When my dad called, I decided I'd go to the chapel and pray the Divine Mercy chaplet for my grandfather.

The following morning, my dad called again to let me know that my grandfather had died. When I asked at what time my grandfather had passed into eternity, my dad told me that it had been 11:00 pm central time. That was precisely when I had finished the Divine Mercy chaplet. No one in the family had been with him just then because they were sure he would make it through the night. I truly believe that in some special way I was present to my grandfather as I prayed the chaplet in the presence of the Blessed Sacrament. In those final hours, I believe, he hadn't been left alone.

Louise H., Alabama

Sixteen years ago I had a lonely and frightful summer as I underwent a clinical trial of chemotherapy for stage 2 breast cancer. The treatment had severe side effects. I was extremely weak and had so little energy I could do nothing more than lie down or sit all day. I was alone at home most of the time. The only prayer possible for me during those long days was to meditate on Jesus in agony in Gethsemane the night before he died on the cross. In my imagination I placed myself next to Jesus while the apostles slept. Here I found peace as I imagined myself holding Jesus' hand and keeping company with him as he was overwhelmed by his coming betrayal, crucifixion, and death. It occurred to me that the apostles may have been allowed to fall asleep so others like myself could keep watch with him. This simple prayer of keeping company with the Lord turned a depressing and lonely time into a moment of grace and peace.

Grace D., Minnesota

When I was eighteen years old, I made a Cursillo retreat that changed my life. On the last night of the retreat, I went to confession. I then felt as if a roadblock between me and God had just been lifted, and I was finally able to look at him without any guilt or fear. I went before Jesus in the tabernacle and offered a prayer of thanks. Kneeling in the pew, however, I began to feel that I had forgotten something. Searching my mind and heart, I prayed, "Lord, did I forget something? I feel like something is still aching in my heart, something I am not seeing. Show me, Lord. What is it?"

In my heart I felt the Lord's reply, "Dustin."

Dustin! Inwardly I cringed at his name. Dustin had committed a grave crime against me—rape. For two and a half long years I had carried the pain and humiliation, the anger, the low self-image that all began that awful night. Not only had Dustin sexually assaulted me, he taunted me about it at school and on the bus. Young and immature, I did not know what to do, how to get away from him, or where to get help.

The memory of that horrible night lived on, tearing my heart and soul like a thousand knives. I could not get away from it. Drowning in pain, not able to breathe, my chest hurt, quite literally. How could I go to God, feeling worthless as I did? I could never get there to the Fountain of Mercy on my own. I could not walk anymore; shame weighed me down. The pain of that night, the memory of it all was suffocating me. But my Mother Mary carried me. She lifted me to the fountain of Christ's mercy, gently, and showed me I did not have to be ashamed of something that was not my fault.

So when the thought of Dustin came looming up again, I immediately felt the same rush of fear I had felt that night. Timidly I prayed, "What about him, Lord?"

"Forgive him," the Lord whispered in my heart.

My chest tightened and I squirmed, "Lord, I don't know. I don't think I can. That's asking an awful lot, Lord."

He replied, "Look up, Grace." At this, I lifted my eyes from the tabernacle where our Lord resided and looked up to the large wooden crucifix suspended over the altar. "Look at me. I just forgave you all the sins you have ever committed, and they were many. I died for you because I love you, and all those sins are forgiven … gone. And now, you say *I* am asking a lot? Don't you think *you* are asking a lot? I forgave you all your sins in confession just now, and you ask me to withhold forgiveness from him. Aren't *you* asking an awful lot?"

That was hard to hear. But I realized the Lord was challenging me out of love, so that I could be free of any resentment and hate. If I let those feelings into my heart, they would end up destroying me. To forgive Dustin did not mean that his crime didn't matter, but that I had to leave him to God. Despite my feelings of fear, I said immediately, "Okay. Yes, Lord. Yes, Lord. I forgive him." I have never felt God smile like I felt a smile pass across my soul that day. Never have I felt such quiet and peace flood into my unhappy soul. All my self-loathing, all my lack of self-worth were repaired, just gone. I was whole. I felt new and happy, and—dare I say it?—holy. I felt all of this because God helped me to let go of the pain, fear, betrayal, and desolation caused by what Dustin had done to me. In forgiving him, I found a vast peaceful fountain springing up in me, flowing from the merciful and loving heart of my Savior, Jesus. Loving and living, God lived in me … *me!* I was incredulous with joy and dizzy with gratitude. I had carried such a heavy burden for so long that it nearly killed me. I was finally free of all of that desolation and destruction. For the first time I could breathe, I could live. I would then begin my journey of a life in Christ, a life full of the merciful love of Jesus, my Lord.

Mary Ann T., New Jersey

My mother was on a respirator, and the doctor told us her prognosis was very poor. He suggested that we should honor her advance medical directives and take her off the respirator, letting nature take its course. Although I knew we were not morally obliged to keep her on artificial life support, the idea of making such a decision was agonizing and deeply emotional for me.

The night before we were to make the decision, I left my mother's side and went to the chapel and fervently prayed to Jesus the Divine Mercy. I begged our Lord to spare my mother from any additional suffering, and to spare us from having to make a decision regarding the respirator. When I returned to her room, I noticed a change in her. My mother's eyes were fixated upward and would not close. She extended her hand out to me, and held onto my hands as though someone was reaching out for her.

I left the hospital that evening and the next morning we did have the respirator removed. She died peacefully less than thirty minutes later. I am confident that Jesus answered my prayer. Our Lord extended his love and mercy to my mother and my family by quickly taking her home.

ANNA N., MASSACHUSETTS

For more than fifty years, I struggled with a poor self-image that sometimes went to the point of self-loathing. I prayed constantly to be freed from this. About two years ago, I was waiting in line for confession when I felt the Lord's closeness to me. The following words suddenly came to my mind: "Don't you realize that if you continue to allow this self-loathing to rule your life, you are denying the presence of the Holy Trinity within you?" This moment of grace changed the way I looked upon the Lord, and I finally allowed his great love and mercy to enter my being.

Sister Christine S., Massachusetts

Several years ago I had sinus surgery, which required my first overnight stay in a hospital. I was anxious and scared beyond words, especially because I would be alone. Then I thought of my youngest sister, whose husband had stayed with her all night when she was in the hospital. I turned to Jesus and told him that he was my Spouse, so I had every right to ask him to stay with me just as my sister's husband had stayed with her. (I've always been a bold prayer!)

When the day of the surgery came I still felt some anxiety, but I truly believed that Jesus would be there for me. He "came" just as the anesthesiologist approached me. A sudden and intense sense of peace and serenity flooded my being. It stayed with me in the moments before the surgery in the operating room, during recovery, and especially during that long night. I simply knew that Jesus was there beside me. I have never experienced the Lord's presence as I did during that time.

Joseph K., Florida

For twenty-five years my family had lived on Pensacola Beach, Florida. My wife and I had raised our children there, and we had established long-lasting friendships. But then Hurricane Ivan crashed into our lives. We were able to evacuate to safe ground and weathered the storm. At first we thought that we would be gone for a week at most, but this hurricane caused more damage than others we had lived through. We couldn't return home for over a month.

When we were finally allowed to go back home, we found that almost everything we owned was gone. The porch from the house next door had hit our living room extension, opening up a huge gap through which all our furniture and appliances had been sucked out. All the windows on the ocean side had been shattered.

As we searched through the rubble, we found bits and pieces of items that had once adorned our home. We especially searched for a six-foot Sacred Heart statue that had weathered all the previous storms and had become a "member of the family," enthroned in a place of honor. The storm had shattered the statue, but then we found the one piece that meant so much to us—the heart. It had not been broken. We were thrilled. My family still has the heart of the statue of Jesus inside a clear case. It is a sign to us that "deep waters cannot quench love." Jesus helped us through the difficult months and years of piecing our life back together. We told people, "we really didn't lose anything in the hurricane because we still have everything that is most important to us: our faith, our family, and our friends!"

Madonna J., California

My mother always had a devotion to the Sacred Heart of Jesus and trusted in his loving mercy. At one point she befriended a neighbor, Anne, who had a difficult and unhappy life. Anne struggled with alcohol and drugs, and this led to her divorce. She remarried, but only to find herself in another unhappy marriage. When my mother befriended her, Anne was in her late sixties, and she had been away from the Church for most of her adult life.

Besides encouraging Anne to return to the Church, Mom prayed constantly for her. After Anne's second husband died, Mom introduced her to the Divine Mercy novena, which they prayed together. That year, on the Feast of Divine Mercy, Anne received the sacrament of Reconciliation and returned to an active life in the Church. Less than a month later, Anne died. During her last days she was at peace and radiated an inner peace and joy.

George M., Missouri

When I was eighteen, I traveled to Sydney, Australia to participate in World Youth Day. It was an amazing experience, full of prayer, fellowship, and the excitement of traveling to a foreign land.

Ever since I was twelve or thirteen years old, I had struggled with same-sex attraction. I hadn't confided in anyone about my struggle, and it was becoming an increasingly difficult cross to bear. The atmosphere of fellowship with the other pilgrims at times added to my struggle, as we grew closer as friends. I was guarded in my actions, however, for fear of revealing that I was attracted to the other guys.

In Sydney, we were hosted by a beautiful Croatian parish, which also hosted a large group of

Polish pilgrims, including some Sisters of Our Lady of Mercy (Saint Faustina's order associated with devotion to the Divine Mercy). One day, the Sisters of Mercy conducted an all-day Divine Mercy devotion. My pilgrim group and I stayed to pray the chaplet in the evening, then left.

Later that night, feeling deeply isolated and stressed, I walked back to the parish, where the sisters were reading passages from Saint Faustina's diary aloud. I knelt down in the Church, with my head and shoulders sagging under the weight I bore. I felt I could not bear this cross any longer. My heart cried out to the Lord, "Why? Why must I bear this cross? Why must I go through this pain?" Immediately after this cry of my heart a young sister read a passage in which Our Lord said to Saint Faustina, "The suffering soul is closest to my heart." Tears flowed, but tears of gratitude and joy that the Lord had seen fit to answer my question in such a beautiful way.

Every day that thought helps me in my struggle to remain chaste and follow the Lord through the teachings of his Church. I again felt the Lord's mercy reaching out to lighten the load at the most recent Courage Conference. (Courage is a group of Catholics with same-sex attractions who desire to follow the Church's teachings, remain chaste, and draw close to Jesus.) A fellow attendee gave me a beautiful booklet on the Divine Mercy. Through these experiences I have come to understand the Lord's mercy in an indescribably intimate way. So let all of you who suffer, be it from same-sex attraction or any other cross, know that we who suffer are closest to Jesus' heart, and let us cry out with Saint Faustina, "Jesus, I trust in you!"

Joanna P., Oregon

One day my sister Julie called me to say that her husband was thinking of divorcing her to marry another woman. He wanted to leave the children with Julie. As she told me this, her sobs wrenched my heart as much as they did hers. She deeply loved her children and still loved her husband. In ten years of marriage she had survived her husband's two affairs and immature demands. My heart broke for her as she sobbed, "What will happen to the kids?"

My parents and the rest of our family poured out a tremendous amount of love and respect for Julie. She tried to mend the relationship with her husband. When she asked him to try and make things work out at least for the sake of the children, he responded with the painfully cutting words,

"I'm sure you'll be okay. I'll stick around until you're on your feet." So quietly and peacefully they separated. The children remained with Julie, who had to find a job to support them, and her husband left for another woman. The children could spend their time with either parent as they desired.

Shortly afterward, Julie's husband was diagnosed with a terminal illness. He had less than a year to live. The woman for whom he had left his wife preferred her freedom and left him. Now he was alone. Julie struggled over what she should do. Through all the pain of her husband's decision to leave her, she had still loved him. Despite his rejection, she had waited, hoping for the day when he might return. Now it looked as if that could never happen. Her girls would be raised without a father.

As her husband grew weaker and had to stop working, Julie saw him become a lonely man unable to care for himself. She started bringing meals over a couple of times a week. Later she took the kids over to help her clean the house. Eventually she took him into her home to care for him in his final months.

I asked her how she could do it. She told me that although he had hurt her deeply, she had decided not to hurt him back. She had asked God to let her be a channel of mercy in the world, and that included being a channel of God's mercy toward her husband. She said she felt richly repaid, as the last few months of their life together were marked by reconciliation and repentance and an intimacy that she had never expected. Mercy had called forth mercy.

Melissa J., Alaska

When I was in high school, I came home one day and sat down at our round study table to enjoy some quiet. As I sat there I suddenly had a sense that my father's life was in danger. (This had never happened to me before and has never happened since.) I was so certain that my dad was going to die that I started to plead for God's mercy on him, because I knew my dad was not ready to go to meet God. I didn't know what was happening at the time, but he had been very angry and seemed unhappy. I found out later that he had been seeing another woman.

I decided to call my mom at work to ask her to pray with me for Dad. She assured me she always prayed for him, but I insisted that she stop whatever she was doing to pray for dad right away. Even if it was brief, I told her, it had to be real. So she did.

I hung up the phone and continued to pray through tears and grief. A few moments later, I had this deep feeling of being heard by a God who loved my father infinitely more than I did or ever could. I felt God's mercy in that moment in such a profound way. I knew that he understood my desire for my dad's happiness (and ultimately eternal happiness) from the depths of my heart—a daughter's heart. All I could do was offer prayers of praise and thanksgiving.

That evening I heard my father say to my mother, "I had to swerve like mad to avoid that accident." Several cars had crashed in a deadly accident on the highway and my father, through the mercy of God, had escaped.

Katie J., Massachusetts

A friend shared with me her concerns about Rachel, a woman she had known for many years. They had grown up and gone to school together, and had been friends as young adults. Later they had drifted apart as they each chose different paths in reference to God. Now Rachel was dying of inoperable cancer in another state. My friend was worried about her salvation, because Rachel had stopped practicing any religion and almost seemed to hate God. Rachel made it clear that she did not want to see a priest and refused the last sacraments.

I led my friend in a prayer of inner healing for Rachel. We closed our eyes and took Jesus to her bedside. We asked Jesus to heal each stage of Rachel's life, and in particular whatever led her to reject God. At the end I asked my friend what Jesus was doing. "Jesus is leaning over Rachel and giving her a blessing."

When I saw my friend a week later, she said, "Some interesting things are going on with Rachel.... She has started talking about a picnic that she is supposed to be going to. She says her grandfather and her sister (both of whom had passed away years ago) are setting up the picnic. She even knows what food will be served. She's going to have a large glass of ice-cold soda. But she keeps on saying that something is holding her back from going to the picnic, and she doesn't know what it is. She still won't allow a priest to visit her."

I knew immediately that this picnic was not just a fancy of her imagination. We were on holy ground, and I wanted to bow down in adoration of a God who could so creatively pursue Rachel. My friend continued, "The hospice says they don't understand why she is still alive. She has no blood pressure. Her organs are shutting down. She just keeps talking about this picnic she is supposed to go to." God was not going to let Rachel die without trying every possible avenue to get to her heart.

"I know her family won't let you come to see her," I told my friend, "but if you can get someone to put a phone to her ear, lead Rachel in an act of perfect contrition. Don't use the formal prayer, but lead her in an act of sorrow in the context of her picnic."

My friend called Rachel immediately. She was sleeping, but she got her mother to put the phone to Rachel's ear. "Rachel, I know you want to go to this picnic that everybody in heaven is preparing for you. Now it's time to go, but first tell God that you are sorry for anything in your life that you may have done that was wrong. Just say, 'O God, I am sorry for my sins with all my heart. I love you. I want to come to you. I trust you. Amen.'"

Rachel died a few days later. At the funeral, Rachel's brother took my friend's hand and thanked her, saying, "I want you to know that Rachel made peace with God before she died. I know that you wanted that, and I want to tell you that it's okay now. She was at peace when she died."

Prayers

I will sing of your might; I will sing aloud
of your steadfast love in the morning
For you have been a fortress for me
and a refuge in the day of my distress.
O my strength, I will sing praises to you,
for you, O God, are my fortress,
the God who shows me steadfast love.

— Psalm 59:16–17

PRAYERS TO THE SACRED HEART OF JESUS

First Friday Devotion

Through Saint Margaret Mary, Jesus requested that we honor his Sacred Heart, especially on the first Friday of the month, by fervently receiving Holy Communion and offering reparation for sins.

The Twelve Promises of the Sacred Heart

The following are the principal promises that Jesus gave to Saint Margaret Mary for all those devoted to his Sacred Heart:

1. I will give them all the graces they need for their state of life.

2. I will give peace in their families.

3. I will console them in their troubles.

4. I will be their refuge in life and especially at the hour of death.

5. I will bless all their undertakings.

6. Sinners will find in my heart the source and infinite ocean of mercy.

7. The lukewarm will become fervent.

8. Fervent souls will grow in perfection.

9. I will bless those places where an image of my Sacred Heart is exposed and venerated.

10. I will give to priests the graces needed to touch the most hardened hearts.

11. Persons who promote this devotion will have their names eternally written in my heart.

12. In the abundant mercy of my heart, I promise that my all-powerful love will grant to all those who receive Communion on the first Fridays of nine consecutive months the grace of final repentance. They will not die without receiving the sacraments, and my heart will be their secure refuge in their last hour.

This last promise requires that the person receive Communion devoutly with the intention of making reparation to the Sacred Heart of Jesus and of obtaining the fruit of this great promise, while living out his or her baptismal commitment throughout life.

Prayer of Trust by Saint Margaret Mary

O Heart of Love, I place all my trust in you. Although I fear my own weakness, I hope all things from your goodness.

Act of Consecration of the Family to the Sacred Heart

The Lord Jesus has promised to bless families consecrated to his Sacred Heart: "I will bless those homes where an image of my heart is displayed and venerated. I shall give peace in their families. I shall bless all their undertakings. I shall be their safe refuge in life and especially at the hour of death."

To make this consecration, obtain an image of the Sacred Heart of Jesus that has been blessed by a priest, and display it in a prominent place in your home. After the image has been set in place, the entire family will pray aloud the act of consecration. This consecration can be renewed on solemn feasts such as Christmas, Easter, Corpus Christi, and of course the Sacred Heart.

Making the enthronement to the Sacred Heart in the home means that we recognize the living presence of Jesus, who attracts all the members of the family or group to his Sacred Heart.

More than a veneration of an image or a simple prayer, it is a way of life, a reminder of love, a call to repay Jesus' sacrifice of his life for us with love and joy.

Most loving heart of Jesus, you gave Saint Margaret Mary the consoling promise that you would bless those homes in which an image of your Sacred Heart is displayed and venerated. We ask you today to accept the consecration of our family to you. By this act we intend to solemnly proclaim your kingship over all creation and acknowledge your kingship over us. O Jesus, reign over our family and over each of its members. Reign over our minds that we may always remain steadfast in the truths you have taught. Reign over our hearts that we may always follow your teachings. O Divine Heart, you alone are our loving Redeemer, for we have been purchased at a great price, your own precious blood.

Uphold your promise, Lord Jesus, and grant us your blessings. Bless us in our labors, in our undertakings, in our health, and in our interests. Bless us in joy and sorrow, in prosperity and in adversity, now and always. Grant that peace may reign among us, and allow harmony, respect, mutual love, and good example to direct our every action.

Preserve us from danger, grave illness, critical accidents, and, above all, from serious sin. Write each of our names in your Sacred Heart and grant that they always remain there, so that after having been united with you on earth, we may one day be united with you in heaven, to sing the glories and triumphs of your mercy. Amen.

Parent: We want God, who is our Father.

All: We want God, who is our king.

Pray one Our Father, one Hail Mary, and one Glory to the Father in honor of the Sacred Heart of Jesus, and a Hail, Holy Queen to the Blessed Virgin Mary to obtain her protection.

Act of Reparation to the Most Sacred Heart of Jesus

Most loving Jesus, whose immeasurable love for humanity is too often returned with negligence and disrespect, we wish to make a special act of homage in reparation for the indifference and pain to which your loving heart is subjected.

We ask pardon for our part in this ill-treatment and affirm our desire to do penance for our personal sins and for the sins of those who have strayed from the path to salvation and no longer follow your law of love and mercy.

It is our intention to offer the satisfaction that you once made on the cross to your Father, and that you renew daily on our altars at Holy Mass. We offer this in union with Mary your Mother and all the saints in heaven. With the help of your grace, we promise to make reparation, as much as we are able, by deepening our faith and observing your law of charity. We promise to do all we can to proclaim your love to others through our witness of holiness and Christian commitment.

Most loving Jesus, through the intercession of the Blessed Virgin Mary, our model in atonement, accept our offering of this act of reparation. Keep us steadfast in your love until the day you bring us home to the happiness of heaven where you with the Father and the Holy Spirit live and reign, God forever and ever. Amen.

For the Church

Jesus, Divine Master, I praise and thank your Most Sacred Heart for the great gift of the Church, which instructs us in the truth, guides us on the way to heaven, and communicates supernatural life to us. The Church continues your own saving mission here on earth as your Mystical Body. It is the ark of salvation; it is infallible, indefectible, catholic. Grant me the grace to love your Church as you loved and sanctified it in your blood. May all sheep enter your fold; may everyone humbly cooperate in your kingdom. Amen.

Blessed James Alberione

Thanksgiving for the Gift of Redemption

Jesus, Divine Master, I praise and thank your most gentle heart, which led you to give your life for me. Your blood, your wounds, the scourges, the thorns, the cross, and your bowed head tell my heart: "No one loves more than he who gives his life for the loved one." Because you died to give me eternal life, I want to spend my life for you. I want you to always, everywhere, and in all things dispose of me for your greater glory. May your will be done in my life. Inflame my heart with holy love, that I may love you always more and love others for your sake. Amen.

Blessed James Alberione

Litany of the Sacred Heart of Jesus

(Approved for use throughout the universal Church by Leo XIII in 1889)

Lord, have mercy on us.
Christ, have mercy on us.
Lord, have mercy on us.

God, our Father in heaven,
have mercy on us.
God the Son, Redeemer of the world,
have mercy on us.
God the Holy Spirit,
have mercy on us.
Holy Trinity, one God,
have mercy on us.
Heart of Jesus, Son of the Eternal Father,
have mercy on us.
Heart of Jesus, formed by the Holy Spirit
in the womb of the Virgin Mother,
have mercy on us.
Heart of Jesus, one with the eternal Word,
have mercy on us.
Heart of Jesus, infinite in majesty,
have mercy on us.
Heart of Jesus, holy temple of God,
have mercy on us.

Heart of Jesus, tabernacle of the Most High,
have mercy on us.
Heart of Jesus, house of God and gate
of heaven,
have mercy on us.
Heart of Jesus, aflame with love for us,
have mercy on us.
Heart of Jesus, source of justice and love,
have mercy on us.
Heart of Jesus, full of goodness and love,
have mercy on us.
Heart of Jesus, wellspring of all virtue,
have mercy on us.
Heart of Jesus, worthy of all praise,
have mercy on us.
Heart of Jesus, king and center of all hearts,
have mercy on us.
Heart of Jesus, treasury of all wisdom
and knowledge,
have mercy on us.
Heart of Jesus, in whom dwells the fullness
of divinity,
have mercy on us.
Heart of Jesus, in whom the Father
is well pleased,
have mercy on us.

Heart of Jesus, from whose fullness
we have all received,
have mercy on us.
Heart of Jesus, desire of the everlasting hills,
have mercy on us.
Heart of Jesus, patient and merciful,
have mercy on us.
Heart of Jesus, generous to all who turn
to you,
have mercy on us.
Heart of Jesus, fountain of life and holiness,
have mercy on us.
Heart of Jesus, atonement for our sins,
have mercy on us.
Heart of Jesus, weighed down with insult,
have mercy on us.
Heart of Jesus, bruised for our offenses,
have mercy on us.
Heart of Jesus, obedient even unto death,
have mercy on us.
Heart of Jesus, pierced by a lance,
have mercy on us.
Heart of Jesus, source of all consolation,
have mercy on us.
Heart of Jesus, our life and resurrection,
have mercy on us.

Heart of Jesus, our peace and reconciliation,
have mercy on us.
Heart of Jesus, victim for our sins,
have mercy on us.
Heart of Jesus, salvation of all who trust in you,
have mercy on us.
Heart of Jesus, hope of all who die in you,
have mercy on us.
Heart of Jesus, delight of all the saints,
have mercy on us.
Lamb of God, you take away the sins of the world,
spare us, O Lord.
Lamb of God, you take away the sins of the world,
graciously hear us, O Lord.
Lamb of God, you take away the sins of the world,
have mercy on us.

V. Jesus, gentle and humble of heart,
R. Touch our hearts and make them like your own.

Let us pray.

Father in heaven, we praise and thank you for the gifts of love we have received from the heart of your Son, Jesus. Teach us to see Christ in those whose lives we touch and to show our grateful love through service to our brothers and sisters. We ask this through Christ our Lord. Amen.

THE DIVINE MERCY

The Chaplet of Divine Mercy

Begin with an Our Father, Hail Mary, and Apostles' Creed.

On the large bead before each decade:

Eternal Father, I offer you the Body and Blood, Soul and Divinity of your dearly beloved Son, our Lord Jesus Christ, in atonement for our sins and those of the whole world.

On the ten small beads of each decade:

For the sake of his sorrowful passion, have mercy on us and on the whole world.

Conclude with (after five decades):

Holy God, Holy Mighty One, Holy Immortal One, have mercy on us and on the whole world *(3 times)*.[6]

6. Sisters of Our Lady of Mercy, *Jesus I Trust in You*, pp. 43–44.

Three O'Clock Prayer to the Divine Mercy

You expired, O Jesus, but the source of life gushed forth for souls, and an ocean of mercy opened up for the whole world. O Fount of Life, unfathomable Divine Mercy, envelope the whole world and empty yourself out upon us. O Blood and Water, which gushed forth from the Heart of Jesus as a fount of mercy for us, I trust in you. Amen.

PRAYERS FOR CONFESSION

Prayer Before Confession

Lord, I kneel here before you and ask you to clear my mind of all distraction so I can spend this time preparing to receive this sacrament of love, healing, and forgiveness. Help me to see how I have offended you and my neighbor. Take away anything that would blur my inner vision so I can confess my sins with a sincere mind and heart. Remove any fears that might prevent truthfulness, and allow peace and trust to enter my being.

Act of Contrition

O my God, I am heartily sorry for having offended you, and I detest all my sins, because of your just punishments, but most of all because they offend you, my God, who are all-good and deserving of all my love. I firmly resolve, with the help of your grace, to sin no more and to avoid the near occasion of sin.

Contrition can also be expressed in your own words, such as:

Jesus, I ask your forgiveness for my sins. I am sorry for offending you. Please help me to avoid all sin in the future.

Act of Hope

O my God, relying on your almighty power and infinite mercy and promises, I hope to obtain pardon of my sins, the help of your grace, and life everlasting, through the merits of Jesus Christ, my Lord and Redeemer. Amen.

Act of Love

O My God, I love you above all things, with my whole heart and soul, because you are all-good and worthy of all love. I love my neighbor as myself for the love of you. I forgive all who have injured me, and I ask pardon of all whom I have injured. Amen.

How to Go to Confession

Preparation

Before celebrating the sacrament of Reconciliation, take some time alone and ask the guidance of the Holy Spirit as you examine your conscience. You can use the Ten Commandments, the Beatitudes, and the examples of Jesus as a guide. You could also ask God to show you what he has been doing in your life and what he is asking of you. Think about Jesus' love for you, and tell him how sorry you are for your sins. Decide what changes you need to make so as to avoid sin in the future.

Going to Confession

After the priest welcomes you, both of you make the sign of the cross. Then you may wish to indicate facts about your life and how long it has been since your last confession.

The priest may read a scriptural passage.

Confess your sins. The priest then offers suitable advice and imposes an act of penance, usually a prayer, act of self-denial, or work of mercy.

The priest invites you to pray a prayer expressing your sorrow. You can use the traditional act of contrition or a prayer of contrition in your own words.

The priest extends his hands and pronounces the formula of absolution, making the sign of the cross over your head during the final words. You answer, "Amen."

The priest will lead you in a proclamation of praise for the mercy of God, such as "Give thanks to the Lord for he is good," to which you answer, "and his mercy endures forever."

The priest dismisses you and bids you go in peace.

After Confession

Perform the penance you have been given. You may also pray a prayer of thanksgiving.

In Thanksgiving for a Good Confession

Dear Lord, I thank you for this wonderful sacrament, through which you have forgiven all my sins and faults. Beyond all doubt, you are a generous and gracious God whose mercy is limitless. Thank you for giving me this fresh start. Grant me the graces I need to walk the straight and narrow road. When temptations come, help me to resist them. But if I fall again I know that you will always be there to lift me up, dust me off, and gently point me in the right direction. Thank you for loving me and letting me experience the peace that only you can give me.

PRAYERS TO JESUS MASTER

Appeals to Jesus Master

Jesus Master, sanctify my mind and increase my faith.

Jesus, teaching in the Church, draw everyone to your school.

Jesus Master, deliver me from error, from useless thoughts, and from eternal darkness.

Jesus, Way between the Father and us, I offer you all and await all from you.

Jesus, Way of sanctity, make me your faithful imitator.

Jesus Way, render me perfect as the Father who is in heaven.

Jesus Life, live in me, so that I may live in you.

Jesus Life, do not permit me to separate myself from you.

Jesus Life, grant that I may live eternally in the joy of your love.

Jesus Truth, may I be light for the world.

Jesus Way, may I be example and model for souls.

Jesus Life, may my presence bring grace and
consolation everywhere.

Prayer to Become Like Jesus

Jesus Master, you have words of eternal life.
Replace my thoughts with your thoughts,
I want my thinking to be influenced by
your teaching;
I want to make decisions according to
your standards.
You are the Truth given to me by the Father.
Live in my mind, Jesus Truth!
Your life is the Way—certain, unique, true,
the way of love for the Father,
the way of love for others to the point of
total sacrifice.
Grant that I may understand your way.
At every moment, may I follow you,
and may I refuse to follow
every way that is not yours.
What you want, I want; give me your will
in place of mine.

Jesus, substitute your heart for my heart.
With your divine life, illumine my life.
You say, "I am the life." Therefore, live in me.
May your life be evident in my own living,
just as happened with Saint Paul, who said,
"Christ lives in me."
Live in me, Jesus Master, Way, Truth, and Life.

Blessed James Alberione

Prayer for True Freedom

Jesus Divine Master, you have called us to yourself and have inserted us into your covenant of love. You are our Master, the Way, the Truth, and the Life. All history finds complete fulfillment in you. Through the action of your Spirit, configure us to your mystery of death and resurrection, and allow us to say with Saint Paul, "I live now not with my own life but with the life of Christ who lives in me." Help us to live in true freedom, and guide us to respond to your call to holiness of life, thereby becoming with you, way, truth, and life for our brothers and sisters. Amen.

Margaret Edward Moran, FSP

Prayer for a Good Life

Divine Master, the time will come when we must leave this life. May we run the race; may we reach the finish line; may we keep the faith; may we find waiting for us the prize of victory given for a good life. You, the just judge, will give it to us on that day, and not only to us, but to all those who wait for you to appear. In your promises, Lord, we find safety and hold firmly to the hope placed before us. Be the anchor of our lives and give us the courage to go on, hoping that where you have gone we shall also go. Amen.

Margaret Edward Moran, FSP

Hour of Eucharistic Adoration [7]

For the grace to trust in the love of Christ

Introduction

Saint Paul powerfully expresses what Christ's love means to him in the Letter to the Romans. Paul faced tremendous obstacles in preaching the

---

7. Cf. Marie Paul Curley, *Life for the World: A Way of Eucharistic Adoration for Today* (Boston: Pauline Books & Media, 2002), pp. 99–106.

Gospel, and by his martyrdom he gave the ultimate witness to Christ. His relationship with Christ gave Paul the security to risk everything for the sake of the Gospel.

Adoring Jesus Truth

Read Saint Paul's Letter to the Ephesians 1:3–23, which reveals the depth of a true relationship and complete dependence on Christ.

Reflection

Christ reveals his love for us in innumerable ways: creating us, blessing us with every spiritual blessing, choosing us in love to be holy, embracing us as his brothers and sisters, redeeming us, promising us eternal life.... What is the most powerful way that you have experienced Christ working in your life? Is there a phrase in this reading that helps you to realize in a fresh way God's overwhelming love for you?

Following Jesus Way

As graced as we are, we know that we do not trust enough in the Lord's goodness and love for us. Learning to trust in God is a lifelong journey. Read the passage from Mark's Gospel that relates the moving story of how Jesus restored life to Jairus' young daughter. Use it to reflect on the ways God calls us to trust (Mk 5:21–24; 35–43).

What are your deepest fears? How do they prevent you from acting out of love? How would a greater trust in the Lord change your life?

We pause to reflect on the challenges we face in our daily lives, especially our fears, and confront them with the words and example of Jesus.

Pray this prayer adapted from Paul's Letter to the Romans as an act of trust in God's tremendous love for you:

If God is for us, who can be against us?

If God didn't spare his own Son but instead gave him up for all of us, won't he also freely give us everything along with his Son?

Who will accuse God's chosen ones? God himself pardons them!

Who will condemn them? Christ died and rose for us and is now at God's right hand interceding for us!

Who or what will separate us from Christ's love?

Affliction, distress, persecution, famine, destitution, danger, or the sword?

[Add your own fears here—be as specific as you can.]

In all these things we are winning an overwhelming victory through the One Who loved us.

We are convinced that neither death nor life, neither angels nor principalities, neither things present nor to come, nor powers, neither height nor depth, nor any other created being will be able to separate us from God's love in Christ Jesus our Lord (based on Rom 8:32–39).

Sharing Jesus' Life

The following prayer, Creed of the Called, is based on the Pauline letters and focuses on the relationship between the disciple and the Father—how we trust that God will work in and through our lives.

Creed of the Called

We believe that God chose us in him before the world began, to be holy and blameless in his sight (Eph 1:4).

We believe that those whom he foreknew he predestined to share the image of his Son (Rom 8:29).

We believe that God, who had set us apart before we were born and called us by his favor, chose to reveal his Son to us that we might spread among all people the good tidings concerning him (Gal 1:15–16).

We believe that God has saved us and has called us to a holy life, not because of any merit of ours but according to his own design—the grace held out to us in Christ Jesus before the world began (2 Tim 1:12).

We believe that Christ Jesus has judged us faithful and worthy by calling us to his service (cf. 1 Tim 1:12).

We believe that we are apostles by vocation, servants of Christ Jesus, set apart to announce the Gospel of God (cf. Rom 1:1).

Considering our vocation, we believe that God chose the weak of this world to shame the strong, so that our faith would not rest on the wisdom of men but on the power of God (cf. 1 Cor 1:27; 2:5).

We believe that to each one God has given the manifestation of the Spirit for the common good (cf. 1 Cor 12:7).

We believe that we must live a life worthy of the calling which we have received: with perfect humility, meekness, and patience, seeking to grow in all things toward him (cf. Eph 4:1–2).

We believe that all things work together for the good of those who love God, who have been called according to his decree (cf. Rom 8:28).

We believe in him whose power now at work in us can do immeasurably more than we ask or imagine (cf. Eph 3:20).

We believe that he who has begun the good work in us will carry it through to completion, right up to the day of Christ Jesus, because he who calls us is faithful (cf. Phil 1:6; 1 Thes 5:24).

Convinced that God loves us unconditionally and is always with us, we resolve to take one risk today to more faithfully live out the demands of the Gospel.

Prayer of Presence

We adore you, Jesus,
eternal Shepherd of the human race.
You are present in the Eucharist
to dwell continually in the midst of your people.
You nourish us, you guard us,
you guide us to the heavenly fold.
We do not live on bread alone,
but on your Word of truth and love.
We listen to your voice

and follow it with love.
Give us the grace to listen to and love your Word,
that it may bear fruit in our hearts.
Speak, Lord, your servant is listening.

Blessed James Alberione

TRUST IN GOD'S GOODNESS: A WALKING MEDITATION

The famous saying of Julian of Norwich, "All shall be well," should be a mantra for anyone who worries about doing the right thing, frets over failures, or anguishes over sins. God wants us to delight in him. That is all. He will make everything else "well" for us. This exercise is designed to set you on that path.

1. *Take a walk along a favorite place, a beautiful spot that has revived your spirits in the past, or even along a busy street.* If possible listen to soft, instrumental music during this experience of prayer.

2. *Start to walk slowly and reflectively.* Notice the beauty around you. "All shall be well." Notice the sunlight. "All shall be well." Take note of small animals that play on the ground. "All shall be well." If you pass others on the sidewalk, bless them silently. "All shall be well." If you are walking in a mall, notice the retailers and shoppers. "All shall be well." On a city street congested with traffic, offer to God the hearts of those driving by. "All shall be well." Walk for fifteen minutes or so, with this blessing as a mantra, "All shall be well."

3. Returning home, *enter your special place of prayer.* Let your mind wander. If a worry arises, "All shall

be well." If a resentment surfaces, "All shall be well." If a sin comes to mind, "All shall be well." If a memory intrudes, "All shall be well."

4. *Picture Jesus on the cross.* Offer thanksgiving and praise for this work of love, which surpasses anything we could have hoped for.

5. *Picture God beside you.* Whether you feel good about yourself or not, your life is rooted and grounded in Love. God, in his goodness, which pervades and sustains your existence, simply asks you to rejoice in who he is and forget who you are, losing yourself in your love for him. God longs to bring you into eternal bliss.

6. *Bring to mind your most compassionate image of God along with your deepest worry.* Know that the Lord is with you. If you flee to him, he will comfort you and make you clean, secure, and safe. "All shall be well." End the time of prayer repeating quietly, "All shall be well."[8]

---

8. Kathryn J. Hermes, FSP, *Beginning Contemplative Prayer: Out of Chaos Into Quiet* (Boston: Pauline Books & Media, 2009), pp. 84–85.

PERSONAL INTERCESSIONS FOR MERCY

For Newlyweds

Most Sacred Heart of Jesus, you have promised to bless those families who honor you by placing your image in their homes. As we begin our life together, we ask your blessing as we journey together through life as a couple. Through your Heart, may our hearts remain as one, always filled with a pure and selfless love. May that love increase throughout the years and remain always new.

For Those Who Worry About Salvation

Dear Jesus, you died for my sins so that I may someday rejoice with you in an eternity of peace and love. Help me to believe ever more profoundly in your Divine Mercy so that I may be freed from the burden of worrying over eternal salvation. Open my heart and mind so that I will never again doubt your infinite love and forgiveness.

To Accept Oneself

Jesus, help me to accept myself as I am, with my good traits and my shortcomings. I want to experience your love, as well as the love of others, but I sometimes find it difficult to love myself. Take away this stumbling block, and let me truly know and feel the depth of the love you freely want to give me. To truly love my neighbor, I must learn to love myself. When I start to be drawn into self-loathing, help me to look up to you and listen to the healing word you will speak to my heart.

Prayer to Become a Merciful Person

Lord, sometimes I am too quick to judge others and speak harsh, hasty words. Help me to show the same mercy and kindness to others that you have so often shown to me. As I want to be loved and treated with compassion, let me extend love and compassion to others.

When I Am Feeling Loneliness

Dear Lord, I am so alone. I feel so empty and cold, for it seems that everyone has abandoned me. I sometimes even doubt that you are there. Please come quickly to my aid. I implore you to bring me the warmth and fullness of your Sacred Heart. Let me know that you are near to me. Return hope to my troubled soul, and let me again believe in your love and presence.

How Have I Spent My Life?

My life is passing me by. I am troubled by some of the things I've done (or haven't done). I am so afraid of being judged for my actions or lack of action. Calm these fears, which are troubling my mind, body, and spirit. Father of Mercy, flood my anxious being with your peace and love, and allow me to trust and believe in you.

For a Spouse/Child Away from the Church

Jesus, you see how much I worry about my spouse/child. You have given them the gift of faith. They have had the grace of receiving you often in the Eucharist. But now for whatever reason they are wandering far from you. I know that you are right behind them, but I'm not. Sometimes I get angry. Other times I argue with them. Often I just can't understand why they are looking elsewhere for what you alone can give them. Help me to calm myself. Open my heart to listen with compassion. Teach me to place them patiently and with trust into your kind and strong hands. When I am frightened for them, when I miss them beside me at Mass, be there also for me. Amen.

Intercession for Friends Who Are Away from God

Today, Lord, I am praying to you for my friends. I am trying to trust your divine timing. I am trying to patiently allow their journey to you to unfold. I am trying not to force my belief on them, but rather to offer it as a precious pearl. But it's hard. Help me trust you with all the seasons of their life. Teach me when to speak and when to keep silent. Help me take advantage of the moments when your grace has opened their hearts and to share my life and hope with them simply and truthfully. May I treat them with love and respect, that they might see you when they encounter me. Amen.

A Prayer in Loss

Jesus, I have been wounded by loss. I am trying to "toughen up," but it is not working. Love makes one so vulnerable to loss. Though it is painful, I beg you to expand and soften my heart. I bring my heart to you, and beg you to give me a thousand small gifts in return. Jesus, through the merits of your Most Sacred Heart, which suffered such pain on Calvary, help me to love what I have lost, not to despise it in bitterness and anger. Keep my heart open. Keep it soft. Help me forgive and cherish whoever has caused me this loss. You understand loss, and you alone can transform it into a deeper love. I give you my heart. Amen.

A Prayer for the Good Samaritans Among Us

Father in heaven, your mercy extends over the earth like the rainbow in the sky, through the Good Samaritans among us who risk their lives daily for the safety and health of others. Nurses, police officers, firefighters, doctors, guards, bomb squads, members of the armed forces.... Sometimes I go about my life completely forgetting that others are always there to protect and defend me if I should need it. They are an image of your ever-present, all-embracing care for me. Give them your blessings each day. Make them wise. Strengthen and sustain them, and may they have in heaven the reward you have promised to those who give their lives for another. Amen.

A Prayer for Forgiveness Among Nations

God, make us look to you. Let us see your face and we shall be saved.

Forgive the sins of nations.

Pardon leaders.

Intervene between countries that are fighting each other.

Have mercy on nations embroiled in violence, suffering from corruption, and lacking hope for a future.

Even as we strive to protect our own country, do not let us fail to discover the dignity of other people.

Have mercy on us, O Lord, have mercy on us now and forever. Amen.

A Prayer for God's Mercy on a World that Disregards the Sanctity of Life

For all those who are involved in any way in sins against the sanctity of life, we pray, Lord of life, have mercy.

For the unborn, we pray, have mercy. For those who deny the right to life of the unborn, we pray, Lord of life, have mercy.

For the elderly, we pray, have mercy. For those who would deny the right to life of the elderly, we pray, Lord of life, have mercy.

For the handicapped and terminally ill, we pray, have mercy. For those who would deprive them of life and a future, we pray, Lord of life, have mercy.

For all who suffer in any way at the hands of others who do not respect their right to live, we pray, Lord of life, have mercy.

For all who contribute to violence, injustice, and indignity in the world, who deny people their rights as human beings to a safe and dignified life, we pray, have mercy.

For a world that has systematically deprived millions of their right to life, we pray, Lord of life, have mercy. Have mercy. Have mercy.

For those of us who work to procure the right to life and human dignity for all, we pray, have mercy. For those of us who haven't, for those who have passed laws that endanger the right to life of anyone, we pray, Lord of life, have mercy. Have mercy. Have mercy.

A Prayer for the Strength to Forgive Past Wrongs

My God, I don't know if I will ever be able to forgive. It doesn't seem fair that I must be the one to forgive when I was the one so hurt. Why should I have to bear the results of another's actions and on top of that treat that person with charity and respect? I'm seething with anger. I'm sorry, it just isn't possible. It just isn't right.

(Express to God how you feel as honestly as you can.)

My God, I do not want to waste my life in bitterness. I do not want to harm myself by hatred. For my own sake at least, I need to try to forgive.

Lord, I do not know, nor could I even imagine, what was in the heart of the person who hurt me. I cannot know how he or she has been hurt. Those intentions and desires are hidden from me. I don't know all the extenuating circumstances that created the situation that has marked my life so painfully.

I decide, my Lord, here and now, that I am not going to punish the other person in retaliation. Instead give me the wisdom to look upon that person and on myself with compassion. If speaking or writing to him or her would be fruitful, show me the right time, give me words that are compassionate and truthful. Restore to me a sense of the person's dignity and my own. Help me communicate respect and forgiveness.

I feel a new sense of freedom, a little breathing space, some lightness to the heaviness in my heart. I still feel pain and perhaps always will, but I know I have taken steps toward being a person of integrity. I have done what you would do. I have done to the other what you have already done to me. Amen.

A Prayer for the Strength to Forgive Oneself

Jesus, I have made so many mistakes that I am afraid my life can never be straightened out. Right now I feel tempted to give in to self-loathing and despair, but I know you still look on me with love. Give me the grace to forgive myself and trust in your mercy. Help me to look on myself with compassion, the same compassion with which you hold me always in your Most Sacred Heart. Amen.

A Prayer of Healing and Blessing for Troubled Hearts

Lord Jesus, you came to heal
  our wounded and troubled hearts.
I beg you to heal the torments that
  cause anxiety in my heart.

I beg you in a particular way to heal
all who are the cause of sin.
I beg you to come into my life
and heal me of the psychological harm
that struck me in my early years,
and from the injuries that it caused
throughout my life.
Lord Jesus, you know my burdens.
I lay them on your Good Shepherd's Heart.
I beseech you—by the merits of the great,
open wound in your heart—
to heal the small wounds that are in mine.
Heal the pain of my memories,
so that nothing that has happened to me
will cause me to remain in pain and
anguish, filled with anxiety.
Heal, O Lord, all those wounds that have been
the cause of so much evil that is rooted
in my life.
I want to forgive all those who have
offended me.
Look to those inner sores
that make me unable to forgive.
You who came to forgive the afflicted of heart,
please, heal my own heart.
Heal, my Lord Jesus, those intimate wounds
that cause me physical illness.

I offer you my heart.
Accept it, Lord, purify it, and give me
the sentiments of your Divine Heart....
Make me an authentic witness
to your resurrection,
your victory over sin and death,
your living presence among us.

Mary Peter Martin, FSP

A Litany for Healing and Release

Lord Jesus, you are my Good Shepherd and Healer.

I come to you, the Rock of my salvation, my only hope in the darkness of my weakness.

Place your hand on my heart, calm its beating.

Heal me, Lord Jesus.

Jesus, cast into the sea of your mercy all my negative thoughts.

Jesus, heal my mind.

Jesus, source of peace, you know what disrupts my peace, what unnerves and disturbs me and those around me.

Let the waves of your divine peace wash over me and heal me.

Lord, I cannot concentrate. My fantasy is always in flight.

Hold me still, so I may at least for a moment rest in you and know you better.

Lord, I find myself fidgeting and forgetting about you.

Remind me that you are in charge of my life.

Lord, my horizon is billowing with the darkest of clouds.

Jesus, may your light pierce my darkness.

Lord, I feel so alone. No one seems to truly know what I am going through.

Lord, I trust in you, for you know me more deeply than any earthly lover can.

Memories of past evils haunt me and tell me I am no good.

Cast painful memories away forever and keep me certain that you made me good and that you love me always.

Lord, I fear crowded places, even churches. Others think me strange and antisocial when I panic.

Console and calm me, Lord. Remind me that you are here protecting me.

Lord, violent thoughts rage through my mind, delusions and negativity swamp me.

Reach down and quiet me. Banish these harmful and chaotic thoughts. Send your Holy Spirit to hold and calm me. Amen.

Mary Peter Martin, FSP

Prayer of Longing for Christ

Come, true light.
Come, life eternal.
Come, hidden mystery.
Come, treasure without name.
Come, reality beyond all words.
Come, person beyond all understanding.
Come, rejoicing without end.
Come, light that knows no evening.
Come, raising up of the fallen.
Come, resurrection of the dead.

From a tenth-century prayer to Christ

Afterword

Not an ending but a beginning....

This is your invitation to better know the mercy, kindness, and love of Jesus.

Ask yourself: Who is Jesus for me, right now, at this point in my life?

Have I gone to him when I was weary and my burden heavy?

Have I let him give me rest? Experienced the gentleness of his sacred heart?

Yes, Lord, this is what I want ... for you to walk beside me each day as my Guide, Friend, Comforter, and perhaps even Rescuer.

Let me believe in your absolute forgiveness when I stray from the virtuous path.

Let me believe that you want me to be at peace with myself and others.

Let me believe that yours is a love without limits ... freely given ... no strings attached!

If you have any doubts—listen to Jesus' own words and ponder the depth of his love.

> "As the Father has loved me, so I have loved you; abide in my love."
> (Jn 15:9)

> "No one has greater love than this, to lay down one's life for one's friends."
> (Jn 15:13)

MARY
Help in Hard Times

Compiled and written by
Marianne Lorraine Trouvé, FSP

"Am I not your mother? Do you need anything else?" With these words, Mary was not just speaking to St. Juan Diego, but to the whole world.

As our loving Mother, Mary can help us in all the problems of life:

When illness strikes
When debts pile up
When doubts disturb our faith
When loved ones stray
When the heart seeks solace

Paperback   128 pages
#49391 $7.95 U.S.

ST. JOSEPH

Help for Life's Emergencies

Compiled and Edited by
Kathryn J. Hermes, FSP

Saint Joseph, foster father of Jesus and husband of Mary, is often called on to intercede in the selling of a house. However, those with a devotion to Saint Joseph know that he can help with much more: employment, family issues, happy death, finances, divine providence, home improvement, and good health. Let the stories and prayers in this book help you open your heart to the care that Saint Joseph can provide.

Paperback 128pp.
#71230 $5.95 U.S.

ANGELS
Help from on High

Compiled and Edited by
Marianne Lorraine Trouvé, FSP

Scripture and Tradition guide the reader toward a deeper understanding of the angels and the part they play in our lives as helpers, protectors, and friends. Through stories, prayers, and popular devotions, this book provides inspiration and information based on the teachings and the practices of the Church through the ages.

Paperback 144pp.
#07907 $5.95 U.S.

A mission of the Daughters of St. Paul

As apostles of Jesus Christ,
evangelizing today's world:

We are CALLED to holiness
by God's living Word and Eucharist.

We COMMUNICATE the Gospel message
through our lives and through all
available forms of media.

We SERVE the Church
by responding to the hopes and needs
of all people with the Word of God,
in the spirit of St. Paul.

For more information visit our website:
www.pauline.org.

The Daughters of St. Paul operate book and media centers at the following addresses. Visit, call or write the one nearest you today, or find us at www.paulinestore.org.

CALIFORNIA
3908 Sepulveda Blvd, Culver City, CA 90230 — 310-397-8676
3250 Middlefield Road, Menlo Park, CA 94025 — 650-369-4230

FLORIDA
145 S.W. 107th Avenue, Miami, FL 33174 — 305-559-6715

HAWAII
1143 Bishop Street, Honolulu, HI 96813 — 808-521-2731

ILLINOIS
172 North Michigan Avenue, Chicago, IL 60601 — 312-346-4228

LOUISIANA
4403 Veterans Memorial Blvd, Metairie, LA 70006 — 504-887-7631

MASSACHUSETTS
885 Providence Hwy, Dedham, MA 02026 — 781-326-5385

MISSOURI
9804 Watson Road, St. Louis, MO 63126 — 314-965-3512

NEW YORK
64 W. 38th Street, New York, NY 10018 — 212-754-1110

SOUTH CAROLINA
243 King Street, Charleston, SC 29401 — 843-577-0175

TEXAS
Currently no book center; for parish exhibits or outreach evangelization, contact: 210-569-0500, or SanAntonio@paulinemedia.com, or P.O. Box 761416, San Antonio, TX 78245

VIRGINIA
1025 King Street, Alexandria, VA 22314 — 703-549-3806

CANADA
3022 Dufferin Street, Toronto, ON M6B 3T5 — 416-781-9131